Nan Socolow reaches out to touch places we don't see and yet recognize, and in her simple words, teaches us to pay attention.

—Joan Konner, Dean Emerita
Columbia Graduate School of Journalism

The haiku-like spareness of Nan Socolow's style evokes vivid imagery, fulfilling to perfection Wordsworth's poetic ideal of "emotion recollected in tranquility."

—Sarah-Ann Smith, author
Trang Sen: A Novel of Vietnam

ArsPoetica is an imprint of Pisgah Press, established in 2011 to publish and promote works of quality offering original ideas and insight into the human condition and the world around us.

Copyright © 2016 Anne K. Socolow
Printed in the United States of America

Published by Pisgah Press, LLC
ArsPoetica
PO Box 1427, Candler, NC 28715
www.pisgahpress.com

Book and cover design: A. D. Reed, MyOwnEditor.com
Cover photo of the author by Irina Triasugina.
Cover painting, "Eila's back yard, Cayman Brac," by Petrina Wright.
Used by permission.

All rights reserved. No part of this publication may be reproduced, stored in a retrieval system, or transmitted, in any form or by any means, electronic, mechanical, photocopying, recording, or otherwise, without the prior written permission of Pisgah Press and Anne K. Socolow, except in the case of quotations in critical articles or reviews.

Library of Congress Cataloging-in-Publication Data
Socolow, Anne K.
Invasive Procedures/Nan Socolow

Library of Congress Control Number: 2016952035

ISBN-13: 978-1942016229
ISBN-10: 1942016220
Poetry/philosophy, life, love

First Edition
November 2016

Invasive Procedures

Earthquakes, Calamities,
& poems from the midst of life

Nan Socolow

Acknowledgments

Page 16. "Death of a Divemaster" previously appeared in *Caymanian Compass*, the national newspaper of the Cayman Islands.

Page 28. "Riding into Battle, My Heart on Your Lance" previously appeared in *The New Republic* and Dell Publishing's anthology *Waltzing on Water.*

Page 44. "Declaration" previously appeared in *Washingtonian Magazine.*

Page 85. "Fish" originally appeared in *Rolling Stone.*

Foreword

I have known Nan Socolow since the fall of 1946, when she entered Miss Johnson's fourth grade class at Friends Seminary in New York City; I had been at Friends since the first grade. Thereafter, we were classmates in a very small group that never numbered more than 26 until we graduated in June 1955 and went our separate ways to college.

In the ensuing six decades, I have sporadically stayed in touch with Nan and, for a brief period in the 1980s when she lived in the Washington, DC, area, where I have lived for the past 50 years, we saw each other occasionally; but after she moved first to Princeton, N.J., and then the Cayman Islands, I have really known very little about her activities. I have been aware that she always liked to write, that she was a rather indefatigable sender of intelligent, perceptive, and often very pointed communiqués to *The New York Times* and, in more recent years, to its online version and blog, and that she had occasionally published poetry.

But it has come as a rather astonishing and entirely wonderful surprise to read this book of her poems. I say astonishing because I was totally unprepared for the extent of Nan's talent as a poet. Her command of vivid and evocative imagery—phrases like "painted shutters / alligatored by time" and "Palms samba sway"——combined with her clever and meaningful reworkings of familiar titles and phrases—"a regular playboy of the western whirl," "I can / face the music / if you will dance / the last / dance/ with me," "I'd like to / swing on a star/ carry moonbeams home / in a bucket," and my personal favorite: "What I am looking for / is a tie / that binds / loose"—produces a mixture of the playful and the humorous with a mature and often moving understanding of life's twists and turns.

Nan's subjects—nature, marriage, parenting, aging, death—are those that are part of all our lives; and over and over as I read her poems, I recognized the familiar, always expressed simply and directly but often also with a tinge of irony and a good deal of astute perception.

Nan is as on the mark describing the movement of ants and yellowjackets as she is in providing us with her portrait of two aging fishermen in "Endangered Species," one of my favorite poems in the book. She is as poignant in an elegy like "Death of a Divemaster" as she is humorously self-deprecatory in "Hottie."

Part II of the book, "You may have your way with me," as the ambivalence of its title perfectly suggests, deals often movingly but just as frequently humorously with the many fluctuations, the joys and sorrows, of romance, courtship, marriage, and separation. Throughout this section, as well as in the collection as a whole, I heard the voice of someone who has lived and observed life closely and fully and is expressing through the medium of poetry a wry, sophisticated, and acute understanding of the natural world as well as the human interactions which frequently complicate our understanding of that world.

It will not take you long to read through *Invasive Procedures*; but I can guarantee you that you will want to reread it almost immediately after finishing it. Upon rereading, you will find Nan's deceptively light verse as enlightening and full of wisdom as you will be charmed, amused, and entertained by it.

Jackson R. Bryer
Professor Emeritus of English, University of Maryland

Contents

Part I: My cage door is ajar

Hatchet Time 5
Beckoning 6
Florida Sunrise 7
Birds of a Feather 8
A Suicide 9
Ants I 10
Beachcomber 11
Plaintains 12
Star Light, Star Bright 13
Bird Music 14
The Willow Tree 15
Death of a Divemaster 16
Ants II 17
The Last Yellowjacket 18

Part II: You may have your way with me

Hottie 21
Like Molecules 22
That Ol' Black Magic 23
Saturday Night Sultan 24
You Said 25
Pledge 26
Lakeside 27
Riding into Battle, My Heart on Your Lance 28
All the Women 29
Alpha Male 30
I Want to Grow Old with You 31
Button up Your Overcoat 32
You 33
While Changing Sheets 34
I Saw Your Car 35
Catching My Former Husband Shaving 36
Duck Duck Wolf 38
Dear Sir 39
The Sunday Times 40

Part III: Awesome inventory

How to Catch a Man 43
Declaration 44
The Garbage of My Mind 45
Shopping List 46

Bath Toy	47
Worry City	48
The Fountain Is Dried Up	49
Signs of Age	50
So No More Crib	51
Peach of My Tree	52
Earthquakes, Calamities	53
Cakewalk	54
TKO	55
In Fog	56
Bathed in Salt Water	57
Talk Show Lady	58

Part IV: My naked jaybird soul

In the Midst of My Life	61
The Docktailed Sleek Horses	62
Water Comes to My Eye	63
Secrets of the Good Life	64
Endangered Species	66
Dem Bones	68
Ambulance	69
Biting the Bullet	70
Air Nevada Charon	71
Invasive Procedures	72
Z	73
Mulligans	74
The Distinguished Thing	75

Part V: Dreaming of aqua waters

Undine	79
Life Boat	80
To Market, to Market	81
Dreaming of Aqua Waters	82
For the Time Being	83
Jam on Bread	84
Fish	85
Before the World Wide Web	86
KBO	87
Bodies of Water	88
Lost and Found	90
Alive, Alive-O	92

Introduction

Nan Socolow gives us poems that are short and pert, sweet and sour as if laced with passion fruit. She pounces upon certain moments, capturing them in her net when no one else is looking, as Nabokov captured his butterflies.

In "Air Nevada Charon" we see a young pilot, who looks 12, caught in a blizzard and playing with the instruments somewhere between "his living room" and "Thy Kingdom come." In "Catching My Former Husband Shaving," she revives the undercurrents of their conjugal pleasures in this tableau of a dried and discarded union. He puts on his cologne,

> an arrogant fragrance
> which used to make me
> feel quite faint
> and now just irritates.

Her language is mainly jubilant, exploding into alliteration, old catch phrases, slang of the early 20th century ("bees' knees") or polished French phrases (*de rigueur*) as she plucks images from the air on which she has amply fed, as in the second and final stanza of "Bathed in Salt Water."

> Will death be
> a place of salt
> like the Dead Sea
> or Salton Sea
> atop the
> San Andreas Fault?
> Or will death be
> the Chambre d'Amour
> the Love Bedroom
> of Biarritz?

The staccato beat of the short first six lines comes crashing against the force of the final image—death in the Chambre d'Amour, an inlet of the sea where lovers of old were caught by a sudden tide and drowned.

Nan Socolow's words and music are original and powerful, image and sound playing between past and present, old age and youth, life and death, tragedy and comedy. She offers a delicious feast for readers, particularly those who like their sour with the sweet.

Kathrin Perutz
New York, NY

Apologia

A poem is like a chunk of raw marble. I chip away and chip away at the chunk, and it takes form and becomes far smaller and when nothing further can be chipped away—when only the finest essence of a marble scrap is left—that is my poem. Less is more. On the other hand, Talmudically speaking, sometimes an entire poem will float into my head when I think of an object and it writes itself around that very object. Like a sliver of dried up soap and the poem "Mulligans."

That is how I write poems.

Invasive Procedures

Dedication

This book is dedicated to my children, H. Elisabeth Socolow-Vucinic, Michael J. Socolow, and Jonathan L. Socolow, and their father, Sandy Socolow.

PART I
My cage door is ajar

Hatchet Time

In our
early teen
summers
at the
Clove

    we fed and
    watered
    the chickens
    in their red
    chicken coop.

        White
        Leghorns
        if memory
        still
        serves.

            In the fall
            they lay
            one by one
            on a fat apple
            tree stump.

                And their
                heads,
                bright red combs,
                were lopped off
                sharp-axed.

                    Did you know
                    that chickens
                    really can run around
                    with their heads
                    cut off?

Beckoning

sitting and looking
out my window
at life birding
in the trees
at the blinding sun
setting
at the painted shutters
alligatored by time
a squirrel trembles
leaps legs splayed
and lands safe
on a bobbing branch.
I want to leap
just so.
My cage door is
ajar.
Yet I still whirr
the treadwheel
and barely feel
the beckoning.

Florida Sunrise

At daybreak
an old man
hide tanned brown
makes his lone crabbed way
across the sheared greensward
to the sea.
Bent by age
he might have sat
on a mountain top
or pulled a loaded dray
in another part
of the world.

A yellow schoolbus passes
pinball lights ablink.
Three bicycles
riders martian-helmeted
in aerodynamic plastic
arrow lycra
on the road.
Three pelicans glide above
pterodactyl
in a straight line
beneath dawn's
salmon clouds.

The condo high-rise glints
in the sun's first rays
off balcony rails
and resin chairs.
Palms samba sway
the air a balm.
The square
aqua jewel pool
surface riffled
by salt breeze
old skin
awaits.

Birds of a Feather

I watch her
yellow-crowned
night heron
stalking on the sand
in front of
my window.

She is alien
as a bird can be
under her
fetchingly adorable
fascinator
feathers.

Her bright eyes
survey
the beach
and her
twigthin legs
pick-up stix

propel her
slowly
deliberately
forward and I am
riveted.

Still
I watch till
with the greatest
of bird's ease
she spreads
her wings

and flaps off
flies away
to windward
a grey sword hilt
a distant
letter M.

Under her crown
as under mine
a brain.
Under her breast
as under mine
a heart.

We are alien
to one another
two birds
of a feather
both pulse-bound

by life and breath.

A Suicide

She had

they all said

everything

to live for,

though

they didn't

speak to her

lovely face

when she

was alive.

I am trying

right now

to appreciate

this blue jay

feather

mirror splinter

of today's

stunning

blue sky

before it

spins away.

Ants I

I killed
a formal
phalanx
of ants

   dots
   right
   on my
   kitchen floor

      wiped them up
      into the
      trash
      small war

Beachcomber

In flip-flops
I pick my way
over bleached
coral boulders.
Shells and stones
studding the sand
clink
broken pottery
music
under my
cushioned feet.
Pink-lipped conchs
(looney grins)
tar splashed coconuts
coral fans tangled
in skeletal heaps
dot the rocky shore.
Clouds churn above
unhurried and grave
as galleons
deliberate and
weighty as
pregnant women.
Sandpiper intent
I pocket
sea scoured
baubles
and the
aqua Caribbean
purls, chuckles, shushes
murmurs endless
commentary
keeps me company.

Plantains

Uncombed
wind-fringed

tatterdemalion
plantain leaves

flap and flutter
hefting their

dangling loads
of green bananas

with sweetly
penile grace.

Star Light, Star Bright

I'm a pea
a bean
a shrimp
my neck has
such a crick
from gazing at the stars!

Way up high
in the velvet void
Castor and Pollux
fiercely bright
as lust sparkles
in a darling's eyes

Polaris, the Pleiades
Orion and his dog
the Dippers big and small
stars all
could be après tout
dead as doornails

and these little earth ears
wouldn't hear the news
for trillions of light years
such is the nature of our galaxy
astrophysicists (oglers of
celestial bodies) explain.

Oh, the Milky Way and Mars
are candy bars
and yes, I'd like to
swing on a star
carry moonbeams home
in a bucket.

We peewee earthlings
are less than a wink
a blink a flash
in the pan
a candle
in the wind.

The fact that the stars
are dead and cold
(or so we were told
late in the last century)
doesn't in the least preclude
wishing on them.

Bird Music

A balm
sweet as life
can be
is living
near birds.
Is the berries
is the bee's knees
to see our fine
befeathered
friends
take wing
and soar!

Birds sing
chirp cheep
redwinged blackbirds
all manner of
pterodactyls
fly, fly away.
They wear feathers
they court
they make babies
from eggs.

Unfeathered
but behaired
we soar in
imagination.
We don't sing
bird music
but our brains
are winged!

The willow tree

the tree man said
is half-alive.
It towers gnarled
high above my house.

Half its branches
are dry and clack.

I sprayed it
with insecticide
to kill the borers,
to give it
a little more life.

Arthritic
twisted with
bulbous growths
on graceful limbs,

I weep,
the tree
reminds me of

my old father.

Death of a Divemaster

Past the white-barred
red dive flag
swaying on the sea's
sun-kissed
surface
he tumbled
off the boat
into the embrace
of the blue deep.

Clad in his
scuba armor
air tank a
silver carapace
on his back
visor goggled
a knight
of the sea
he descended.

And passed
vast castles
coral palaces
pinnacles
pillars
barbicans of
the city
beneath
the sea.

Watched by
uncurious eyes
phalanxes of
wheeling
shimmering fish
and sea
creatures
in their
divine element

into the warm
welcoming waters
the womb's
salt safe rapture
he vanished
sank into
the pillowed place
of sea
dreams.

Ants II

Just as I
relentlessly
pursue
random ants

dots right
and crush them
with my
thumb

so am I perhaps
pursued by an
anonymous digit
some call god.

The Last Yellowjacket

The last
Yellowjacket
is buzzing frailly

    And crawling in
    a slow circle
    on the cold bricks

        Trees are bare
        frost
        in the air

        The wasp isn't
        flying daring
        bombing missions

Over the picnic table
summer's
its memory

    I have the choice
    to step on it
    crush it

        Put it out of its
        bumbling misery
        or walk on

            we all have our time
            wasp or woman
            I walk on

PART II

You may have your way with me

Hottie

Armed with that
primordial
female will
to paint my face

I stand absorbed
at this mirror
surrounded by
luscious crèmes

Powders and blush
in dots and jars
masking my self
erotic scents
and nonsense

Sloe eyes
doe bright
amid a cloud of Dior
I limn my mouth

Lipstick red
shiny and moist
as an open wound
as that other one

And become
stunning
exotic
distant
geisha face

Like Molecules

Like molecules
  or dodgem cars

Billiard balls a-click
  upon green baize

We carom off
  one another.

Random snowflake
  fluke

Or some
  godly plot

Pooled as
  spilled mercury.

What odds
  we'd meet?

That Ol' Black Magic

When I stand
near a man

I vibrate
like a stabbed

harpstring
heartstring

wearing
radio static

rug spark
warm hand on a bare back

tuning fork
electricity

Saturday Night Sultan

I was meant to be
the favorite
of a sheik
an emir
in some other age
but you are my
Saturday night sultan
and the random pattern
of moles on your back
is an old map to me.

I'm Scheherazade
of the weekend
movies
Queen Sheba
of Monday night
football
and I've read
your flesh
for a thousand
and one nights.

You Said

I was
irresistible
unforgettable
lovely
every man's
dream

That I wore
envy
like a cloak.

You do have
a way
with words
flatterer.
You may have
your way
with me.

Pledge

Look, man
I swear
no hands

no strings
no ties
I promise

No promises
tomorrows
or babies

I don't want
a thing
just your mind.

Lakeside

Lakeside
in spring
two deer
two ducks
all hopes
aside
we had
wine
damp cheese
bread
and a bite
of each
other.

Riding into Battle, My Heart on Your Lance

You're my peach
  You're my prince
    Pennoned
      Gonfaloned
        Tietacked
          You joust
            Mosey along
              Astride your
                Falcon Steed

              You're my bee
              You're my berry
              My cufflinked
                Charlemagne
                  Of traffic jams
                    And medieval nights
                    The modern day
                  Vassal of
                  Medici me

All the Women

I want
to be
all the women
in your life.

First
last and
all the ones
between.

Knowing
you won't
love me
forever

though you've
ardently
sworn
you will,

you—
bee—
will kiss
other flowers.

And Honey,
other bees
will kiss
flower me.

Alpha Male

I like jewels
stones
bright pebbles.
Diamonds
though are
less to me
than glistening
coquina shells
on a wet
Florida
beach,
or teeth
in the smiling
mouth
of my Alpha wolf
sweetie.

I Want to Grow Old with You

I want
to grow old with you
in my kitchen
in my arms
in my bed.

    I want
    to grow old with you
    and give you
    coffee and the paper
    and do those other
    necessary things
    for decades.

        And dance
        in your memory
        sing
        in your heart
        dazzle
        your dear head
        for decades.

            Failing this
            I would be grateful
            for just a day
            or two
            with you.

Button up Your Overcoat

If I could
button up
your
overcoat
between
your face
and the
rifle fire
I'd stop
time dead
like the
figures
on the urn.
In that
nanosecond
I'd build a
thick wall
of bricks
with my
bare fingers
to keep you
from harm's way,
And we'd sprawl
comfy on the sofa
and hold hands
and listen to
the world is
waiting for the
sunrise, if
I could button up
your overcoat
between your
face and the
rifle fire.

PART II: You may have your way with me

You

You
  read the newspaper
  and remark upon atrocities

    vile endeavors
    murder
    rape
    plane crashes
    famine

  and the like.

You
  casually scan

    obits
    movies
    social tidings

  and flip
  through the ads

    smart clothes
    starving babies.

  Does it never occur to
you

    to put down
    your paper
    rush to me

    to laugh kiss and
    hug me tight

    right now
while we live
and breathe?

While Changing Sheets

    I strip our bed
    peeling off
    pillow cases
    one
    two sheets

rich with our old smell
of lust and comfort
dear as a
dog's own fur.

    Perhaps
    one day soon
    I'll think
    of changing
    beds.

I Saw Your Car

I saw
your car
parked at her place

   like a guppy in seaweed
      and knew you were there

injecting her

   with truth serum

      from your

         interesting

            syringe.

Catching My Former Husband Shaving

There are times
communication
between former mates
is necessary

Formal talks
summit meetings
logistics in re:
The Children

One does not
just walk away
so we phone each other
briefly

Summer lightning
a shared past
intruding upon
our separate presents

He's shaving this morning when I call
all business he says
I'll get back to you
in five minutes

I see him naked at his
besteamed bathroom mirror
stripping wide swathes
of white lather from his cheeks

Stretching the skin
of his face
this way and that
to scrape off the night's whiskers

That stubble used to
rub my face
in a thrilling way
once upon a time

I muse on the forked path we took
we live apart now
unattached
as stranded stones on a beach
He splashes water on his face
towels it dry
his eyes slits
he slaps on cologne

An arrogant fragrance
which used to make me
feel quite faint
and now just irritates

Grit in an oyster
when I catch
a whiff
in some public place

My former husband shaving
I savor this glimpse
of our common past
cunning as a wink.

Duck Duck Wolf

You came

You saw

You pitched
The woo

I bought
The Brooklyn Bridge
From you

A juicy
Sitting duck
Was I
You gobbled
Me up
And gnawed
My bones

Duck duck wolf
You grinned
And went your way

To sell
Another duck

Another bridge

Another day

Dear Sir

Dear Sir:
some time ago
you pierced me
and it has taken
years for the pain
to disappear.

An ache remains
on rainy days
some sunny ones, too
but lately
I've begun
to feel again

and you'll be delighted
to know
it only hurts
a little
when I draw
breath.

The Sunday Times

Walking back from town
with the Sunday Times
I pass you two
lovers by.

You walk entwined
in the thoughtless
cocoon of a
comfy hug.

And barely
see me
a woman alone
clutching her Times.

Be assured
that I've been hugged
and fucked to a
fare-thee-well.

And many lips
have kissed me
here there
and everywhere.

I've reeled
from love and
lollipops, the
sweetest glut.

Picnicked for years
on licit and illicit lunches
raspberries and champagne
and a slick lover in bed.

Eyeing you aslant
I divine you're not aware
that where you are now
I've already been.

Bemused I smile
glancing back
at the two of you
enrapt.

You'll find
that time
changes
everything,

and where
I am now
alone and getting
The Times,

so you
each
one day
shall be.

PART III
Awesome inventory

How to Catch a Man

Polyphrenic
pantastic
you straddle
a dozen worlds.

Girl in every port
Jack of all trades
a regular playboy
of the western whirl.

A bird in the hand
you'll never be
nor sin under
the apple tree

with anyone else but
come to me
beside my sea
and see why

I have the world
on a string
by the
shorts.

Declaration

This must be clear
   that I believe in marriage
   in the piece of paper
   and debts and duties
   and so forth
   set forth
   et cetera

Also this
   that it
   isn't forever
   but then no tie
   that binds
   is

What I am looking for
   is a tie
   that binds
   loose

PART III: *Awesome inventory*

The Garbage of My Mind

The garbage of my mind
is heaped with holey socks

worn out sneakers
clabbered bottles

smelly bibs
sticky nipples

stinky heinies
ordures of toileting

unforeseen
premaritally.

And kitchen middens
of disposable waste

boxes cans
plastic bags

Tops lids peels
and scummy water

swirl opalescent
unecologically

amid my thoughts
of higher things.

Shopping List

I have an awesome inventory
three children

two dogs
two houses

goldfish in a pool
dependent plants

dustmice in every corner
beauty

and when he's in Rome
a loving husband

whose secretary buys me
a Gucci bag.

Bath Toy

My son
in the tub
at bathtime
rocks his
rubber ducky.

His buttocks
pink orbs
his penis
bobs and dances
in the suds.

Laughing lathered
naked and free
he sucks his ducky
while I marvel
at tub edge.

He grows up
and I can't
pay enough
attention
as he grows.

I'd preserve him
water wrinkled
finger and toes
in amber or crystal
if I only could

For one of these
too soon days
my boy will be
some other woman's
bath toy.

Worry City

In the
twos and threes
of the morning

when icy wind
clacks the trees
outside

and moonbeams
and headlights
strobe the ceiling

and I
can't
sleep

my husband
lies snoring
boring

while I lie
rigid
clenched

worry city
ticking
mortal

my mind
neon sign
abuzz

I would
click off
my brain switch

and rest
my sore pachinko
head

and rest
my Times Square
Hong-Kong head

The Fountain Is Dried Up

The fountain
is dried up

Our silences
while driving

are long as
the New Jersey Turnpike.

In our car
we skirt declivities

there are inclines
conversational chasms

Crevasses
wadis gulches

So we drive along
alone together

with our
lonesome heads.

Signs of Age

In my
thirties
signs of age
appear on my
comfortable
bony soft body.

Parallel
ski tracks
wrinkle
my brow
sun lines
star my eyes.

Discernible
freckles
spot the tops
of my lean
capable hands.

I do not view
such signs of life
with alarm while you
still point at me
with pride.

And I can
face the music
if you will dance
the last
dance
with me.

So No More Crib

So
no more crib.

All the screws
are unscrewed

and the crib slats
toothmarked railings

fall into neat pieces
collapse like a

flimsy folding chair
or card house.

All my babies
are in big beds
now.

Peach of My Tree

Peach of my tree
my Amelia Earhart

My daughter
leaving

leans against the wind
walks toward the night jet.

Tall and straight
climbs the metal gangway

Hey, Presto! vanishes
Joanie in the whale

all that's left
on earth of me.

Her face pale smudge
peers through the perspex oval

sees my fingers clinging starfish
to the airport's chainlink fence.

Lights blinking
pilots perched aloft

the plane lumbers pregnant
down the runway

palm trees, fence and me
a second's blur to her.

The jet gathers
hurtles, rises

my blood and bones
Persephone within.

PART III: *Awesome inventory*

Earthquakes, Calamities

Earthquakes
calamities
famine and floods
rumors of war
happen elsewhere
on my TV

On my TV
people with
little
to start with
now have
even less

While I slice
and chop
and sauté onions
to the wails
of disaster victims
somewhere else

The elements
unreal and
real events
pass me by
in my tidy
cocoon life

Only small guilts
stab-making
the sharp knife
blade
slip
and welcome
cut a finger.

Cakewalk

Bucking and winging
we tapped our

twinkle-toed way
through the

Singin' in the Rain
of our marriage.

We danced a lot
and never thought

to sit one out
and talk.

TKO

See us
beat
around the bush
at dinner

never landing
a solid right
to the solar
plexus.

You hit
below the belt
I lead
with my jaw

reeling
undecked
punch drunk
no scars show.

Our
meals are
technical
knockouts.

In Fog

In fog
I watch
and wait
airport uneasy
for his plane
to land.

We fly
our times
no surrey
with the fringe
on top
civilization.

In fog
people fly
and drop
from the sky
some within planes
some without.

Bathed in Salt Water

Bathed in warm
salt water in
womens' wombs
till we opened
our eyes on earth
and wailed
crying
salt tears
for the rest
of our lives.

Will death be
a place of salt
like the Dead Sea
or Salton Sea
atop the
San Andreas Fault?
Or will death be
the Chambre d'Amour
the Love Bedroom
of Biarritz?

Talk Show Lady

I see her
on TV.

She's famous
she's a star

She speaks
she laughs

People clap
and shout.

Unmoved
I sigh.

I knew her
well

once upon
a time

when she
used to tie

her babies
in their cribs.

PART IV

My naked jaybird soul

In the Midst of My Life

In the midst
of my life
I am
wondrous
still breathing
in and out.

I've got plenty
things galore
children and animals
inhabit
in habit
my maelstrom.

My hair and nails
grow
and I wax
thin and fat
by seasons
an organism.

I feel changes
like a
weathercock
and move
in vane
in vain.

At thirty-five
I trust
only
my hands
and head
and what I see,

What I hear
in my ear
taste on my tongue
feel
in my
bones,

What mirror mirror
on the wall
who's the
fairest
one of all
tells me.

The Docktailed Sleek Horses

The docktailed
sleek horses
sweetly race
their husbands'
colors.

Saddles and bridles
of status and means
for better or worse
some high-steppers
some mudders.

Blinkered, confined
and tightly reined
in their racetrack rounds
rarely do they
bolt.

Water Comes to My Eye

Water comes to my eye
when I wake up
in the morning

    and find myself
    still alive
    still ailing.

        Hale, my body
        is limitless.
        Ill, I am confined

            to a corral
            of cannot
                while out there

                can do
                    is broad as
                            M o n t a n a

Secrets of the Good Life

A confession:
that I have loved
and saved
fortune cookie
fortunes
for decades.

In the Year Dot
at age 16 was
my first time
at a
Chinese restaurant
The West Lake
in Westport
Connecticut.

Inside the beige
not so crisp
fortune cookie
my fortune read:
   Two dark men
   will enter your life.
   One soon
   to propose.

Damned if it
didn't happen
just so!

And so I saved them,
oblong strips of
paper enfolding
in the cookies
their little
of the good life,
for decades.
   Success is at your
   fingertips!
   Remain persistent!
and I did.

   Never fear! The end
   of something means
   the start of something
   new!
I feared anyway.

   Your ideas are clever
   and you will be
   rewarded!
Fortune cookie
fortunes hiding
and revealing.

Anticipation, aspirations
> You will travel to many
> exotic places in the
> next few years!

dreams
> Wealth awaits you
> very soon!

and philosophy
> Bread today is better
> than cake tomorrow!

A happy jolly fortune
(and a favorite):
> Just to be alive
> is a grand thing!

Or a bitter one:
> You will die alone
> and poorly dressed.

And even Mrs. Malaprop:
> Everything happens
> for a resin!

A confession
(yes, another):
A handsome
Alpha Wolf
used to write me
his own fortunes
on little oblong
pieces of paper.
They were too
ferociously risqué
and ribald to
mention here,
but, oh,

I kept his
happy memories
and home-made
fortunes for years!

Endangered Species

On this barrier beach
Bill and Vince
are old and shrewd
as sea turtles.

These fishermen
in their seventies
were lean and sexy studs
when Kilroy was here.
Bill is wiry
his silver crewcut
neat as a
Blue Jay's crest
His jaunty T shirt
hangs on a lanky frame,
blazons
Babylon Bait & Tackle.
You can just make out
MIAMI in faded leters
on Vince's billed cap
(frayed relic).
Vince is a mechanic
his pitch-scored fingers
fix bikes and
all manner of machines.

The old guys' eyes
are pale as horizons
keen as a wave's
curled cutting edge.
They've seen it, done it all.
Time's bent their spare bodies
into comfy shapes
curved as carapaces.
Vince's heart stopped twice
his skin is cross-hatched
and corded, serviceable
as a retread tire.

PART IV: *My naked jaybird soul*

Bill's meatless bones
have bested cancer.
chemo, cobalt
and his wife's demise.

These old salts
longtime buddies
laugh a lot
and joke,
though these days
one foot's on
a banana peel
and you know
they're hearing
the sirens singing
"September Song"
in the sea's crash dance
on the shingly shore.
Bill says
it takes a helluva lot
to kill a man.
Vince says
doctors don't know
their asses from
a hole in the ground.
Vince and Bill
cackle loud and real
as the wheeling
seagulls above.

Endangered as the dunes
amid pines on this
fragile beach
these old cronies
seize their days
and for now
endure.

Dem Bones

What are those stones
grave stones
head stones
dead people
lie under?

My children ask
fascinated
by cemeteries
as we
drive past.

My interests
lie above
the ground
I sing live bones
your bones.

Ambulance

Keening
down the street
weaving
whipping
sparkling
a pinball machine.

Wailing
whining
ablink
shrieking
attention
must be paid.

Stops traffic
dead
alerts the mind
to now
to the
hereafter.

And we little
curbside
piggies
think
"wee wee wee"
all the way home.

Biting the Bullet

When we reach
the overtime stage of life,
over 70, not golden years,
there is no bible to tell us
what to expect.

And what to do about
the startling aches and pains
that befall our elderly
wellderly illderly bodies.
So we bite the bullet

and tough it out
to avoid
the undertaker's
waiting-room
heebie-jeebies.

Pulling 14
to 16 hour days
was de rigueur
in our thirties and
forties.

And now
in our overtime
we pay for the
crazy dancing
of those days.

In this vale of tears
weltschmerz and
sporadic joys
are the coins
of our realm.

Air Nevada Charon

He's a stork on slender stems
a prince swinging peril slung
a pilot in turbulence above
this boyish unseen canyons.

(looks 12) The blizzard's fingernails
bash-nosed tap and tick
blue eyed amok on the
eager pup. curved blind perspex.

The plane's Blithe Charon
a gimcrack this Air Nevada jock
a teacup steers his bucking craft
an eggshell on instruments.

between buying the farm Confident,
and our icy fingers. an earphoned godlike kid
We are dangling he's flying his
wobbly as cherries living room

while we consider
to the beat of blood
in our ears
Thy Kingdom Come things.

Invasive Procedures

In for the barium
lower GI
speared and stuck
chicken on a spit
leaking cool
chalky wet
onto the gurney,
The Sixth Fleet
backs into me
Gorgeous pain
I shriek
and swoon!

The doctor
a cute cookie
Hampton-tanned
absent as glass
calls me "Dear".
"Hold still, Dear"
he sighs,
distracted by my
innards writhing on
his wee TV.
"Now roll over
and don't breathe, Dear."

Amok, I bawl
Deaf, he murmurs
"OK, breathe, Dear."
My sharp fingernail
in his indifferent eye
and hey, this guy'd
think twice
before calling me dear.
Silent, I think,
oh you fukken pup
don't dear me
just see me.

Z

The last sight I see
each night
is ordinary.
My lamp, the harp
the shade, the bulb.
I douse the light.
One night, every night
nearer to the big Z.

The fan blades whirr,
the sea's sleepy purl,
the me smell of
pillows, blanket, bed.
Pooped out
I curl like a shrimp
into sleep
in my moon zebra room.

Mulligans

Aging
is an unfamiliar
rite of passage
in our lives
(if we live
long enough).

In our twenties
and thirties
we can't imagine
or foresee youth's
sleek veneer
crazed

leaving the
fine spidery
web of years
on our
kissers,
in our minds.

The long long days
of childhood
are now the
short short days
of our seventies.
Zip! What wazzat?

Imperceptibly,
The fragrant plump
soap bar
devolves
into a dry
latherless sliver.

Hot flames of passion
slacken, disappear.
We blow a few breaths
on the embers to see
if they spurt.
No soap.

This life
sometimes
gives us overtime.
Extra years
but no do-overs.
No mulligans.

The Distinguished Thing

When the time comes
    I shall be happy

To be stripped
    of my body

Like the pea
    its pod

The corn
    its husk

The conch
    its shell

The snake
    its skin

And my jaybird
    naked soul

Weightless
    as thistledown

Will gleefully
    flee

Gravity
    and fly

PART V

Dreaming of aqua waters

PART V: Dreaming of aqua waters

Undine

In the
shower
with water
running down
my Aphrodite
body
troubles
melt away

and I laze
irresponsible
out of
touch
Venus
unreachable
under
the spray.

The phone
may ring
and children
shriek
but I
the naiad
Diana
in a tarn

collect
my self
to start
the day.
A cascade
a cataract
it's raining
it's pouring

a freedom
of wet
a bliss
which
extends
exactly
to the edge
of my towel.

Life Boat

Don't sit in this boat
like old aunties
being propelled
by vague tides.

Grasp oars and pull
and whirl your self
through pools and rapids
and fly and fly!

To Market, to Market

I spend weird
and dreamy hours
in the tank
of the market
like the live
green lobsters
furious faced and calm
in their big glass
water box.

Pushing a wire cart
in the casbah
of the supermarket
I pass transient
edible ziggurats
of chubby fruits
bedewed veggies
rococo produce
yummy glut.

Down around
the byzantine aisles
past bread city
to the syrupy
sounds of odious
piped music
past soaps, soups, soda pops
soldier bottles
hi-ho the dairy-o

Cry havoc
at the meat case
assault and battery
of stretch-wrapped
chicken chunks

crimson beef
raw piggie
bizarre
bazaar.

We are
human groceries
important as
beans and peas
immortal as Tide
and Clorox
ice-cream alive today
midden
tomorrow.

Dreaming of Aqua Waters

Stopped at red lights
in November rain
behind metal toads
in New Jersey traffic
I dream of
aqua waters.

A jet flight,
and hours away
soaring through
the sunny blue
high above
mellow clouds.

And the ocean
down below
thrown
like a bolt
of slubbed
blue silk.

As the green
traffic light
prods me
to GO! GO!
I think,
accelerating

right foot firm
on the pedal
capable gloved hands
gripping the
hard plastic wheel
how simple it would be

to live by the sea
in the warm aqua water
watching silver fish
wheel like
showers of tinsel
flung among coral heads.

For the Time Being

For the time being
I keep a
merry-go-round
in revolution.
Glassy-eyed
my horses
pump wooded on this carousel
swanning calliope
circles.

For the time being
never ending rounds
of painted ponies
duty days
parade abreast
faintly chipped
and tattered
I deliver
food, care
and love.

For the time being
I am dizzy
blinkered
amidst my
whirling horses.
Seeing sky outside
I driven try
to catch
the brass ring
and fly.

Jam on Bread

I would like to be
    a bohemian
    and live in a
    squalid
    little house
    by the river.

Uncombed
    unkempt
    unkept
    and spread
    myself around
    jam on bread

and live by
    the golden rule
    of sloth
    and pledge
    no allegiances
    a care less life.

But I am a rich
    leopard
    and leopards
    cannot change
    their spots
    and in my

undiluted self
    deep down
    I know
    the grass
    is always
    greener.

Fish

Caught a bluefish
in the bay
once.
It flapped
and jumped
pancake on the dock
slimed the boards
soiled itself.

Too late
taking pity
I threw it back
in the bay
where it bobbed
belly up.
Caught a married man
once.

Before the World Wide Web

people on islands
listened to
short wave radio
as life went on
in the outside world.

Bomb blasts in Syria.

Shooters in America.

Havoc in Iraq.

Glued
to the news
of the world
by short waves
fiddling with
the dials on
the magic box
hearing tides of sound
many switches to diddle.

Adjusting antenna
and batteries
treble and bass
fine to a hair.
Then, oh joy,
burbling through
the tulgey ether

Big Ben bonged.

Yankee Doodle crowed.

Midnight arrived in Moscow!

Voices rang!
Jewels of sound
shimmered
dear as water
in a dry country

In the
farthest reaches
of this blue orb.
Respighi's Pines
scintillated
aurally succoring
the ravenous ears of
the island-bound.

KBO

I dearly loved
Winston Churchill

He was
so handsome
when he was young.

I was beautiful
as his New York mother when I was young.

The years transmogrified Winston into a bulldog

(who saved England from the fukken
"Narzis" in World War II).

In a boiler-suit and bowler,
Cigar and brandy
in hand when he was old.

I got old
like Churchill did.

And my mantra is what he said every day—

"KBO,"
The dear old dog reminded us

to Keep Buggering
On and so
I do.

Bodies of Water

Aeons past
before the plates
became continents
when this Earth
was young
bodies of water
encircled
Pangaea.

Now our
blue planet
is a dying zone
a waking
nightmare
pillaged and
plundered,
its watery
places ravaged
by mankind.

Detritus dumped
debris dreck
bottles jars
and enough
plastic to gyre and
gimble and
strangle the
Pacific wabe.

Bizarre fish
Asian snakehead carps
sea lamprey eels
with round
sucking mouths
and razor sharp

teeth encroach
in the freshwater
Great Lakes and
mighty Mississippi.

Lionfish
from the Indian
and South
Pacific oceans
loosed from
American aquaria
gauzily dressed
to kill in
fetching saris
swirl *en masse*
in the Caribbean Sea.

Pythons, boas
gators lurk in the
marshy sawgrass
of the Everglades,
eyes aslit for innocent
passers-by
to squeeze and
swallow.

The five continents
that were once one
Pangaea, connected
jigsaw puzzle pieces
like the carapace on a
hawksbill's shell
are now apart
and prisoned by
waste waters.

Billions of people
dying for a taste of
their birthright
of potable water.
Global warming
climate change
inconvenient truths
of our lives on Earth,
truths denied by
some who buy
and chugalug
clean, birthright water
in billions of little
plastic bottles
that will remain
on Earth
long after
we've gone.

Lost and Found

Rumors that Noonan
and I were buried
on Saipan or Tinian
that we were
spying for America
before Pearl Harbor

Beheaded
at Garapan
by the Japanese...
False rumors
urban legends
all

Noonan and I
just glided
from the sky
Out of fuel
we dropped
from the clouds

Past Howland
onto a Phoenix isle
in Kiribati
Nikumaroro
known then as
Gardner Island

My Lockheed
Electra
landed hard
on the atoll's
sharp shallow
reef

I was 39
that day
2 July 1937
and I did so radio Itasca!
Radioed Itasca
over and over!

They searched
every dot and cranny
for Noonan and me
Except for Gardner
the obvious spot
350 miles from Howland

The day we fell
I was 39 years old
five-eight tall
fair and freckled
gaptoothed
small shoe size 6

PART V: *Dreaming of aqua waters*

Cat's Paw heel
The Press
called me
"Lady Lindy"
but they never got
the story straight

Noonan and I died
marooned
needles in a haystack
And the story hung
by a thread
the thread of

Just a leaf
overturned
in the island underbrush
by a hermit crab
revealing the Cat's Paw
heel of my shoe

I would have been lost
gone with the wind
forever
my poor bones
were sent to Fiji
(and "misplaced" there)

Sic transit
Gloria
Mundi
Sic transitted
my Lockheed
10 Electra
My DNA awaits discovery
on Nikumaroro

Buried bits of my plane,
my heel and smashed jar
of Dr. Berry's Freckle
Ointment, too

Noonan and I
went the way of all flesh
on 24 July 1937
my 40th birthday
no cake or candles
or balloons

But isn't it swell?
Isn't it nifty?
This news
that the seekers
will find me this July?
Or maybe next year?

Alive, Alive-O

My
   West is West life
   is riotously peopled
   a gorgeous
   English garden
   a kaleidoscope of
   cockle shells
   silver bells
   and brass bands
   of kinfolk, friends
   children,
   burdens.

My
   East is East life
   is an idle
   seascape
   lone as
   breeze blown curtains
   fleeting as I'm
   forever blowing
   bubbles
   an oyster place

Self
   the pearl.

PART V: *Dreaming of aqua waters*

About the Author

Nan Socolow, born in New York City, studied poetry at Connecticut College with Pulitzer Prize-winner William Meredith (U. S. Poet Laureate, author of *Wreck of the Thresher*), and at Princeton University with Theodore (Ted) Weiss, founder and editor of *Quarterly Review of Literature*. She also studied French Literature at La Sorbonne, Université de Paris, France.

Ms. Socolow served as an officer of the U. S. State Department (Language Services) and U. S. Information Agency (USIA) in the 1980s. She was named Director of Development at Ford's Theatre in Washington, DC, and was the first Administrator of Rockefeller College at Princeton University.

From 1988 to 2014, Ms. Socolow lived in the Cayman Islands, 90 miles south of Cuba, where she worked as a condominium manager, hotel administrator, and real estate agent. She returned to the states, settling in West Palm Beach, Florida, in 2014.

Also available from Pisgah Press

Mombie: The Zombie Mom — Barry Burgess
$16.95

Letting Go: Collected Poems 1983-2003 — Donna Lisle Burton
$14.95
Way Past Time for Reflecting
$16.95

Musical Morphine: Transforming Pain One Note at a Time — Robin Russell Gaiser
$17.95

MacTiernan's Bottle — Michael Hopping
$14.95
rhythms on a flaming drum
$16.95

I Like It Here! Adventures in the Wild & Wonderful World of Theatre — C. Robert Jones
$30.00
LANKY TALES
Lanky Tales, Vol. I: The Bird Man & other stories
$9.00
Lanky Tales, Vol. II: Billy Red Wing & other stories
$9.00
Lanky Tales, Vol. III: A Good and Faithful Friend & other stories
$9.00

Red-state, White-guy Blues — Jeff Douglas Messer
$15.95

A Green One for Woody — Patrick O'Sullivan
$15.95

Reed's Homophones: a comprehensive book of sound-alike words — A.D. Reed
$17.95 hardcover/$10.00 softcover

Swords in their Hands: George Washington and the Newburgh Conspiracy
$24.95 — Dave Richards
Finalist in the USA Book Awards for History, 2014

Trang Sen: A Novel of Vietnam — Sarah-Ann Smith
$19.50

THE RICK RYDER MYSTERY SERIES — RF Wilson
Deadly Dancing
$15.95
Killer Weed
$14.95

To order:

Pisgah Press, LLC
PO Box 1427, Candler, NC 28715
www.pisgahpress.com

www.ingramcontent.com/pod-product-compliance
Lightning Source LLC
Chambersburg PA
CBHW071529080526
44588CB00011B/1601